Rescue and Prevention: Defending Our Nation

- Biological and Germ Warfare Protection
- Border and Immigration Control
- Counterterrorist Forces with the CIA
- The Department of Homeland Security
- The Drug Enforcement Administration
- Firefighters
- Hostage Rescue with the FBI
- The National Guard
- Police Crime Prevention
- Protecting the Nation with the U.S. Air Force
- Protecting the Nation with the U.S. Army
- Protecting the Nation with the U.S. Navy
- Rescue at Sea with the U.S. and Canadian Coast Guards
- The U.S. Transportation Security Administration
- Wilderness Rescue with the U.S. Search and Rescue Task Force

RESCUE AT SEA WITH THE U.S. AND CANADIAN COAST GUARDS

CONTENTS

INTRODUCTION

September 11, 2001, saw terrorism cast its lethal shadow across the globe. The deaths inflicted at the Twin Towers, at the Pentagon, and in Pennsylvania were truly an attack on the world and civilization itself. However, even as the impact echoed around the world, the forces of decency were fighting back: Americans drew inspiration from a new breed of previously unsung, everyday heroes. Amid the smoking rubble, firefighters, police officers, search-and-rescue, and other "first responders" made history. The sacrifices made that day will never be forgotten.

Out of the horror and destruction, we have fought back on every front. When the terrorists struck, their target was not just the United States, but also the values that the American people share with others all over the world who cherish freedom. Country by country, region by region, state by state, we have strengthened our public-safety efforts to make it much more difficult for terrorists.

Others have come to the forefront: from the Coast Guard to the Border Patrol, a wide range of agencies work day and night for our protection. Before the terrorist attacks of September 11, 2001, launched them into the spotlight, the courage of these guardians went largely unrecognized, although in truth, the sense of service was always honor enough for them. We can never repay the debt we owe them, but by increasing our understanding of the work they do, the *Rescue and Prevention: Defending Our Nation* books will enable us to better appreciate our brave defenders.

Steven L. Labov—CISM, MSO, CERT 3

Chief of Department, United States Search and Rescue Task Force

Left: A Coast Guard diver jumps from a Dolphin helicopter into the North Atlantic to rescue a survivor.

ORIGINS OF THE COAST GUARD

On May 26, 1913, an Act of Congress created the Coast Guard by combining two existing federal agencies, the Revenue Cutter Service and the Life-Saving Service. In ensuing years, three more maritime services were incorporated into the Coast Guard. The Steamboat Inspection Service and Bureau of Navigation became part of the Coast Guard in 1936 and the Lighthouse Service was incorporated in 1939.

Though the Coast Guard is a 20th-century organization, the agencies that comprise it are almost as old as the United States itself. On August 4, 1790, Alexander Hamilton, the first secretary of the treasury, created a "system of cutters," later named the Revenue Service, and then the Revenue Marine, then finally, the Revenue Cutter Service. The Coast Guard can thus claim to be older than the United States Navy. The Continental Navy (as it was first known) was disbanded after the Revolutionary War and Congress did not form a new navy until March 27, 1794, after the establishment of the United States.

Left: Cadets graduating from the Coast Guard Academy in New London, Connecticut. The Academy was founded in 1876, with an intake of six cadets, and now graduates 175 cadets every year.

The Dungeness Lighthouse, located at the tip of Dungeness Spit near Port Angeles, Washington. It was the first lighthouse in Puget Sound, established in 1857, and automated in October 1976.

AIDS TO NAVIGATION

On August 7, 1789, the first Congress, in one of its first acts, **federalized** the existing colonial lighthouses and raised funds for more lighthouses, beacons, and buoys. In 1820, the first lightships came into service. The Lighthouse Service built over 1,000 lighthouses and maintained 120 lightship stations around the United States. It fell under the jurisdiction of, first, the Treasury Department, then the Commerce Department, before finally being transferred to the Coast Guard in 1939.

LAW ENFORCEMENT

On August 4, 1790, Secretary of the Treasury Alexander Hamilton created a fleet of 10 cutters to enforce the new **tariff** laws imposed by the United States. These laws were controversial. In colonial days and during the Revolutionary War, seamen who ignored King George's trade laws had been hailed as patriots, but now, the new government needed trade revenue to survive. The tariffs did not go unchallenged. In 1832, South Carolina tried to avoid payment, and President Andrew Jackson dispatched five cutters to Charleston Harbor to intercept foreign ships and assist in collecting revenues.

Protecting tariffs also meant fighting piracy, a practice that continued well into the 19th century. In 1819, the cutters *Alabama* and *Louisiana* captured a ship belonging to an agent of the infamous Jean LaFitte of New Orleans, and went on to capture the pirate stronghold of Patterson's Town on Breton Island. In 1822, Louisiana assisted the Royal Navy and U.S. Navy in capturing five pirate ships in the Caribbean.

HOLEWOOD AND THE TEXAS RANGER

The Coast Guard had many run-ins with liquor smugglers during Prohibition, but none were so daring as the crew of the Canadian vessel *Holewood*.

The Canadian rum-runner *Holewood* took on half a million dollars' worth of liquor at Saint Pierre Island and ran down the coast to a point off New York. There, her crew camouflaged her to look like the well-known U.S. coaster, the *Texas Ranger*. *Holewood* steamed, disguised, through the Verrazano Narrows, past New York City, and on up the Hudson. It was reported as the *Texas Ranger* by maritime observers.

However, a vigilant Coast Guard officer detected the fraud when he saw a shipping news bulletin that reported the *Texas Ranger* in the Gulf of Mexico that day. The Coast Guard overtook *Holewood* near Haverstraw, New York, about 30 miles (48 km) north of New York. The captain and crew escaped in a boat, but were later captured by Coast Guard officers. A search of the ship revealed the liquor, the Coast Guard's most valuable single catch at that time.

In the 1920s, the Coast Guard was charged with enforcing **Prohibition** and embarked upon the "Rum War at Sea." At first, the Coast Guard was unprepared and hampered by a lack of ships. "Rum rows"—lines of ships carrying liquor—were able to anchor offshore, and fleets of fast boats supplied the nation's ports.

In the 13 years of Prohibition, there were some notable encounters, such as the battle with the Canadian ship *I'm Alone* in 1929.

In 1790, Alexander Hamilton, the first secretary of the treasury, established the fleet of revenue cutters that was to become the modern Coast Guard. It was the United States' first maritime force.

Here, the forlorn crew of the schooner, *I'm Alone*, languish behind bars in New Orleans after their ship was sunk by the U.S. Coast Guard cutter *Wolcott* in 1929. The rum-smuggling ship had refused to surrender and tried to evade capture.

I'm Alone was moored off New Orleans with 2,800 cases of liquor on board when challenged by the cutter *Wolcott*. *I'm Alone* fled seaward, pursued by *Wolcott*, who fired across her bows. *I'm Alone* **hove to** for the night, but made off the next morning. *Wolcott*, now joined by the cutters *Dexter* and *Dallas*, gave chase. After repeatedly refusing to heave to, *I'm Alone* was sunk by gunfire from the cutters.

The Coast Guard's law enforcement priorities have changed over the years, reflecting changes in world events. Liquor smuggling ended with the repeal of Prohibition in 1933, and until World War II, the Coast Guard was busy intercepting ships smuggling **arms** to Central America and returning to the United States with narcotics. In 1959, Fidel Castro took power in Cuba, and throughout the 1960s, Coast Guard patrols intercepted the transportation of men and arms, assisted refugees, and maintained neutrality. In the 1970s, drug interception again became important, an emphasis that continues to this day. Priorities have changed again after the terrorist attacks of September 11, 2001, with greater emphasis on homeland security and the interception of arms and terrorists.

ENVIRONMENTAL PROTECTION

The Revenue Cutter Service, and then the Coast Guard, have protected the environment for over 150 years. In 1822, Congress created a timber reserve for the Navy, and cutters were dispatched to prevent the cutting of live oak on those lands.

The purchase of Alaska in 1867 added to the Revenue Cutter Service's ecological responsibilities. At the time, Alaskan fur seals were being hunted into extinction, with a quarter of a million killed in the first four years of American control. At first, Congress restricted the numbers that could be killed. Then, starting in 1874, Revenue Cutter Service personnel camped on the Pribilof Islands to protect the seals' breeding grounds. In 1908, the Service was authorized to enforce all Alaskan game laws.

Protection of fish stocks began in 1885, when the Service

cooperated with the Bureau of Fisheries in the "propagation of food fishes." In 1905, cutters enforced the regulations governing the landing and sale of sponges in the Gulf of Mexico.

The Refuse Act of 1899 was Congress's first attempt to address the growing problem of water pollution and was jointly enforced by the Revenue Cutter Service and the Army Corps of Engineers. There were modifications to the water pollution laws in the 20th century, culminating in the tough new laws of the 1972 Federal Water Pollution Act, enforced by the Coast Guard's Marine Environmental Protection program.

In 1973, the Coast Guard created a National Strike Force to combat oil spills. There are three teams, based on the East, West, and Gulf coasts. These teams have been deployed

The Lyle Gun is used to fire a safety line from the shore or a rescue ship to a ship in distress. Since its invention in the 1870s, it has saved hundreds of lives.

THE LYLE GUN

The Lyle gun, named after its inventor David A. Lyle, is a mortar, or cannon, that fires a line to a distressed ship. Although firing devices had been used since 1800, they were often dangerous or unreliable until Lyle developed his gun in the 1870s. The same basic design of this gun is still in use to this day.

Once the line was secured, survivors were hauled to safety in a breeches buoy or life car. Breeches buoys are lifebuoys with rigid canvas breeches attached, for hauling in one person at a time. Life cars are covered, watertight boats that can hold several people.

Lyle guns were used in two separate rescues in a storm of September 1888. The crew of Hunniwells Beach Station, Maine, rescued 15 people stranded on Glovers Rock. Dangerous rocks prevented the lifeboat from approaching too close, so the crew lashed a Lyle gun to their deck and fired it to reach those in danger. A breeches buoy could not be used because of the rocks, so a small **dory** was rigged to haul the people to safety. During the same storm, the crew of the Lewes Station in Delaware fired their Lyle gun from the upper window of a fish house and landed the crew of a shipwrecked craft into the loft with a breeches buoy.

worldwide to hundreds of spill sites.

The Coast Guard's environmental duties expanded again in 1976, when the Fishery Conservation and Management Act created a 200-mile (322-km) fishing limit, quadrupling the area patrolled by the Coast Guard.

SEARCH AND RESCUE

Federal responsibility for search and rescue began in 1831, when Secretary of the Treasury Louis McLane directed seven cutters to cruise the coast in search of persons in distress.

At the time, search and rescue was organized by individual states. Each state appointed local "wreckmasters" to organize the salvage of goods from shipwrecks, and many of these wreckmasters also assembled volunteer rescue crews whenever a wreck occurred.

In the mid-19th century, most wrecks happened when storms blew immigrant ships bound for New York onto the New Jersey shore. In 1848, the Revenue Marine built two lifesaving stations, one each on the New Jersey and Long Island coasts. Each station was equipped with an iron boat on a wagon and a set of lifesaving equipment, including a mortar for firing lines to ships, a "life car," **breeches buoy**, stove, gunpowder, lanterns, and fuel.

The success of the venture was shown in 1850, when the British vessel *Ayrshire* grounded in a snowstorm on Squan Beach, New Jersey. A volunteer crew assembled by wreckmaster John Maxon rescued 201 of the 202 people on board by firing a line to them and hauling in the survivors in a life car.

In the 1870s, the Life-Saving Service was expanded beyond New Jersey and Long Island. In 1874, stations were built in Maine, Virginia, and North Carolina, followed by more on the Atlantic coast and Florida, the Gulf of Mexico, the Great Lakes, and, eventually, the West Coast and Alaska.

By the turn of the 20th century, improved construction and navigational aids meant fewer passenger ships were wrecked, and coastal search and rescue concentrated more on small sailing craft. At the same time, the Service expanded its coverage with new "blue water" cutters that could reach ships in distress in the Atlantic. Ocean stations were set up in the mid-Atlantic and later in the Gulf of Mexico and the Pacific Ocean.

In 1920, the Coast Guard made its first use of a borrowed Navy biplane, and by the 1930s, amphibious aircraft were offering support to cutters. During World War II, the Coast Guard developed the helicopter for antisubmarine warfare, and after the war, the helicopter became a vital component in search-and-rescue operations, as it remains today.

The sinking of Titanic on her maiden voyage in 1912 with the loss of 1,500 lives prompted Congress to tighten the regulations on shipboard lifesaving equipment and vessel inspections.

In October 1980, helicopters carried out one of the Coast Guard's most celebrated deep-water rescues. The Dutch cruise ship *Prinsendam* was crippled by explosions in the engine room while 200 miles (322 km) off Sitka in the Gulf of Alaska. In strong winds and rough seas, four Coast Guard, one Air Force, and two Canadian Air Force helicopters plucked over 500 survivors from lifeboats and transferred them to the waiting cutter *Boutwell* and the commercial tanker *Williamsburgh*. Not one life was lost.

PREVENTIVE SAFETY

Congress made no provision for maritime safety until 1837, when the steamboat *Pulaski* exploded in North Carolina with the loss of 100 lives. Congress passed an act "for the better security of the lives of passengers," starting commercial-vessel inspections and requiring ships to carry firefighting and life saving equipment. The rules were not enforced, however, and inspection was tainted by corruption. In many cases, inspectors had business interests in the shipping companies and declared unsafe ships to be seaworthy.

It was not until seven steamboat disasters occurred in 1851 and 1852, costing nearly 700 lives, that Congress introduced the Steamboat Inspection Act of 1852, which controlled inspections and licensing. Vessel certification was extended, and life saving devices were improved after the loss of 1,500 lives on *Titanic* in 1912. A number of acts followed in the 20th century, gradually strengthening safety regulations. Although maritime safety is constantly being improved, history shows that it often takes a disaster to prompt Congress to introduce new regulations.

Here, a life boat is moored at the Canadian Coast Guard station at Tofino on Vancouver Island, British Columbia. The Canadian Coast Guard was first established in 1962. Today, it employs over 4,000 personnel and is supported by an auxillary of 5,000 volunteers.

STRUCTURE AND MISSIONS

The Coast Guard is a unique federal agency. It is one of the five U.S. armed forces, and is under the control of the Department of Transportation—although it falls under the control of the Navy in time of war or when the president directs. As well as national defense, the Coast Guard has a broad range of regulatory, law enforcement, humanitarian, and emergency-response duties.

The Coast Guard is responsible for the safety of U.S. inland waterways, ports, and harbors, 95,000 miles (152,980 km) of coastline, U.S. territorial seas, the 3.4 million square miles (9,067,357 sq km) of ocean in the U.S. Exclusive Economic Zone (EEZ), and international waters and other maritime regions of importance.

The Coast Guard is a large and complex organization, but it is flexible, with a good deal of overlap from one mission to another. This is the Coast Guard's main strength. As a unified agency controlling all U.S. maritime interests, the Coast Guard might, for example, board a ship for a safety inspection, only to discover drugs or arms. Similarly, **interdiction** of immigrants from Cuba can turn into a search-and-rescue operation if their flimsy boat runs into trouble.

As its motto declares, the U.S. Coast Guard is

Left: A Coast Guard diver comes to the surface after checking a buoy chain. Verification of navigational aids is an essential part of the Coast Guard's maritime safety operations.

A DAY IN THE LIFE OF THE U.S. COAST GUARD

Responsible for an area of 3.4 million square miles (9,067,357 sq km), the Coast Guard has 35,000 members on active duty, 8,000 reservists, and 32,000 auxiliarists. On an average day, they will:

• Conduct 109 search and rescue cases; Save 10 lives

• Assist 192 people in distress

• Protect $2,791,841 in property

• Seize 169 pounds (77 kg) of marijuana and 306 pounds (139 kg) of cocaine, worth $9,589,000

• Seize one drug-smuggling vessel every five days

• Investigate six vessel casualties involving collisions or groundings

• Process 238 seaman licenses and documents.

In addition:

• Small boats undertake 396 missions

• Aircraft fly 164 missions, logging 324 hours, of which 19 hours are flown off patrolling cutters

• Law enforcement teams board 144 vessels

• Cutter and small boat crews interdict and rescue 14 illegal immigrants

• Marine safety personnel open eight new cases for marine violation of federal statutes

• Marine inspectors board 100 large vessels for port-safety checks

• Pollution investigators respond to 20 oil or hazardous chemical spills totaling 2,800 gallons (10,598 liters).

An injured woman is unloaded from a Canadian Coast Guard rescue hovercraft near Vancouver City, British Columbia. Built in Britain, the CG-045 has been used by the Canadian Coast Guard since the 1970s.

"Semper Paratus"—Always Ready—to fulfill its goals of ensuring safety, guarding the economy, and protecting the environment. The scope of the Coast Guard can be seen in the diversity of its five main missions—maritime safety, maritime mobility, maritime security, national defense, and protection of natural resources.

MARITIME SAFETY

Maritime safety includes the following esential services: search and rescue, marine safety, recreational boating safety, and international ice patrol. Search and rescue (SAR) is probably the best-known mission area of the Coast Guard. In 2000, the Coast Guard

This is the seal of the Coast Guard's Junior Reserve Officers Training Corps. High school students can join the JROTC to learn discipline, marching, and basic Coast Guard training.

responded to over 40,000 calls for assistance, ranging from recreational boaters in distress to freighters sinking in gale-force winds.

The Coast Guard is a recognized world leader in SAR. Whenever the alarm sounds, the Coast Guard is ready to spring into action to save lives. The Coast Guard works closely with federal, state, local, and foreign agencies to provide the best response to distress calls. It also maintains a vessel-tracking system that covers the globe, letting it divert the nearest commercial ship to render assistance.

The Coast Guard's marine safety program promotes safety at sea through its regulation and inspection of vessels. The Coast Guard inspects both U.S.- and foreign-registered ships. Ninety-five percent of merchant ships that call on U.S. ports are foreign.

Maritime safety is not limited to commercial vessels. Over 76 million recreational boaters use U.S. waterways each year. Assisted by the 35,000-person strong Coast Guard Auxiliary, the Coast Guard's recreational boating safety program provides free safety courses, boat inspections, and verification of navigational aids.

MARITIME MOBILITY

Maritime mobility includes the following areas of responsibility: aids to navigation, icebreaking services, bridge administration, and vessel traffic/waterways management.

The Coast Guard is charged with ensuring a safe and efficient marine transportation system. It regulates and inspects commercial and private vessels, licenses merchant ships, manages waterways, and protects the security of U.S. ports. The Coast Guard's aids to navigation program and vessel traffic services ensure safe passage, not only for the 13 million Americans involved in shipping-related activities, but also for the 134 million U.S. and foreign passengers using U.S. waters.

Keeping the marine transportation system running is of great economic importance. More than 25 percent of U.S. domestic trade moves by water, and shipborne trade contributes an annual $740 billion to the U.S. economy. Maritime mobility is also essential for the safe storage and transport of **materiel** sent to overseas conflicts.

MARITIME SECURITY

Maritime security is one of the most dangerous areas of responsibility, and includes: drug interdiction, alien migrant interdiction, EEZ and living marine resource, law/treaty enforcement, and general maritime law enforcement.

The Coast Guard is the only federal law-enforcement agency with **jurisdiction** in U.S. waters and on the high seas. The Coast Guard's enforcement of U.S. laws and international treaties includes conducting counter-drug operations, interdicting illegal immigrants

A Coast Guard Dolphin MM65 helicopter. Helicopters were first developed by the Coast Guard for antisubmarine patrols during World War II and are now an essential part of search-and-rescue missions.

and **contraband**, protecting living marine resources, and intercepting arms and weapons of mass destruction.

The Coast Guard's aim in drug interdiction operations is to detect, disrupt, and deter smugglers and to seize any illegal drugs found. In the fiscal year 1999 alone, the Coast Guard seized more than 11,000 lbs (4,990 kg) of cocaine, keeping some 500 million "hits" of the drug off U.S. streets.

With its long coastline, the United States is vulnerable to illegal immigrants attempting to enter the country by sea. Between 1980 and 2000, the Coast Guard interdicted more than 290,000 immigrants from 44 countries. The Seventh District, covering Florida, the Caribbean, and Puerto Rico, is the busiest in immigrant interdictions. As economic, cultural, and political strife continues around the world, the United States can expect no let-up in these numbers in ensuing years.

The U.S. Exclusive Economic Zone (EEZ) holds 20 percent of the world's fishery resources and supports a commercial industry valued at over $25 billion. The Coast Guard's boarding and inspections of U.S.- and foreign-flagged boats are essential in helping to rebuild and maintain fish stocks depleted by overfishing.

NATIONAL DEFENSE

The Coast Guard services combine with the armed forces and police services in fulfilling the following areas of responsibility: general defense duties, homeland security, port and waterways security, and polar icebreaking.

The Coast Guard maintains a constant state of readiness to

function as a specialized unit of the Navy in time of war and to respond quickly to peacetime crises and conflicts. The Coast Guard is ideally placed to respond to threats, because of the missions it is already carrying out—protection of U.S. ports and waterways, assistance in humanitarian aid, maritime interdictions, and cooperation with other nations in enforcing **UN** treaties and sanctions.

In major-theater warfare, the Coast Guard's tasks include port safety and security and the transportation and protection of forces and weapons. In war, the Coast Guard also has command of the

On September 26, 2001, the Coast Guard cutter *Juniper* anchors off Liberty Island in New York Harbor, monitoring vessel traffic following the September 11 terrorist attack on the World Trade Center.

THE NEW NORMALCY AND OPERATION NOBLE EAGLE

" 'The New Normalcy' for the Coast Guard will mean a higher tempo than existed on September 10 and somewhat lower than the tempo we have known since September 11."

Admiral James Loy, Coast Guard Commandant

The events of September 11, 2001, significantly changed the Coast Guard's mission activity. In the immediate aftermath, cutters, boats, and aircraft were diverted from other activities to concentrate on homeland security, and reserve and auxiliary personnel were immediately called up.

Since then, the Coast Guard has settled into the "New Normalcy"—a heightened state of alert that will continue indefinitely. The Coast Guard's task is to assess potential dangers and identify the unlawful without disrupting the normal free flow of commerce.

More than 35,000 members of the military reserves, including 2,000 from the Coast Guard, have been called to active duty as part of Operation Noble Eagle. This is the name given to homeland defense and civil-support operations in response to the terrorist attacks. The reservists are engaged in port security; medical, engineering, and civil support; and in homeland defense. Many Coast Guard reservists have been assigned to Port Security Units, often carrying out armed patrols. Their duties include protecting the 90 port and waterway areas designated as "security zones," where ship traffic is prohibited.

U.S. Maritime Defense Zones, with ultimate responsibility for protecting the U.S. coastline from attack.

Since the terrorist attacks of September 11, 2001, the Coast Guard's homeland security role has escalated and it has become a vital component of Operation Noble Eagle. The Coast Guard is at a heightened state of alert, protecting over 350 ports and 95,000 miles (152,979 km) of coastline, while maintaining its role in keeping U.S. waterways secure for marine commerce and recreation.

PROTECTION OF NATURAL RESOURCES

In protecting the natural resources of the United States, the Coast Guard covers the following duties: marine pollution education, prevention, response, and enforcement; foreign vessel inspections; living marine resources protection; and marine and environmental science.

The Coast Guard's protection, enforcement, and response tasks in marine environmental protection help reduce the amount of pollution entering America and the world's waterways. The Coast Guard is an acknowledged leader in the field and advises and trains other nations in environmental protection.

The Coast Guard's environmental protection role is of significant importance to the economy. Clean water is vital to the $25-billion U.S. fishing industry. Coastal tourism and marine recreation—

Right: Coast Guard Commandant Admiral James M. Loy shakes hands with a Coast Guard member during his inspection of security operations in New York City after the September 11, 2001, attacks.

worth more than $70 billion—also demand clean shorelines. The Coast Guard's prevention of oil spills saves nearly $6 billion each year in commercial losses and environmental damage.

When prevention and enforcement fail, the Coast Guard is ready to respond to spills anywhere on U.S. coasts and inland waterways. Three National Strike Teams—located in Mobile, Alabama; San Francisco, California; and Elizabeth City, New Jersey—are trained to respond to major oil and hazardous material spills, such as the massive Exxon *Valdez* spill in Alaska in 1989. Post-September 11, 2001, these strike teams are also on alert to deal with any future chemical or biological attacks by terrorists.

THE STRUCTURE OF THE COAST GUARD

The Commandant of the Coast Guard is based at Coast Guard Headquarters in Washington, D.C., where all Coast Guard operations worldwide are coordinated. At the next level of command, the Coast Guard is divided into the Atlantic and Pacific areas, each with its own command and logistics centers. There are also nine U.S. Coast Guard districts.

ATLANTIC AREA

Atlantic Area Command—Portsmouth, Virginia

The Atlantic Area Command Center coordinates homeland security, law enforcement, and rescue missions within its boundaries. It also manages international programs, such as the International Maritime Law Enforcement Team (IMLET) and multinational operations in the Red Sea and Arabian Gulf.

PORT SECURITY UNITS

Coast Guard Port Security Units (PSUs) are staffed primarily with selected reservists. They provide waterborne and limited land-based protection for shipping and critical port facilities in case of need. PSUs are not new, but their role has been extended and new personnel have been trained since September 11, 2001.

PSUs can deploy within 24 hours and establish operations within 96 hours after initial call-up. Each PSU has transportable boats equipped with dual outboard motors and fuel and supplies to last up to 30 days. All PSU staff, whether reserve or active-duty personnel, receive specialized training at the PSU Training Detachment in Camp LeJuene, North Carolina.

PSUs were deployed to the Persian Gulf during Operation Desert Storm in 1990. They also served in Haiti in 1994. In December 2000, PSU 309 from Port Clinton, Ohio was deployed to the Middle East to provide vital force-protection for the Navy assets following the attack on the USS *Cole*.

An armed Coast Guard vessel patrols Boston Harbor. Port security has been increased as part of Operation Noble Eagle, the nationwide program of homeland security.

Maintenance and Logistics Command Atlantic (MLCLANT)—Norfolk, Virginia

MLCLANT ensures the operational readiness of Coast Guard commands in 40 states east of the Rocky Mountains, as well as Puerto Rico, the U.S. Virgin Islands, and Europe. It has over 2,200 personnel, including health, financial, and legal staff. The 1st District is in Boston, Massachusetts, and covers New England, New York, and northern New Jersey; the 5th District is in Portsmouth, Virginia, and covers the mid-Atlantic coast of southern New Jersey, Delaware, Maryland, Virginia, and North Carolina. The 7th District is in Miami, Florida: this is the busiest district, and covers South Carolina, Georgia, the Florida peninsula, Puerto Rico, and the Caribbean. The 8th District is in New Orleans, Louisiana: this is the largest district in the continental United States—it covers Texas, Louisiana, Mississippi, Alabama, the Florida panhandle, and the Gulf of Mexico, plus all other states south of the Great Lakes and east of the Rockies; the 9th District is in Cleveland, Ohio, and covers the Great Lakes and coastal areas bordering the Lakes.

PACIFIC AREA

Pacific Area Command—Alameda, California

The Pacific Area Command coordinates missions in the area and is also headquarters of the 11th District. The region covers the West Coast, Alaska, and Hawaii, and extends from the North to the South poles and across the Pacific to Asia—a total of nearly 74 million square miles (191,709,845 sq km). Missions also include icebreaking in the Arctic and Antarctic, military exercises in Korea and the Middle East, and maritime training in Southeast Asia.

Maintenance & Logistics Command Pacific—Alameda, California
This provides support services for the 8,000 Coast Guard personnel throughout the Pacific Area. The 11th District is in Alameda, California, and covers California, Nevada, Utah, and Arizona; the 13th District is in Seattle, Washington, and covers Oregon, Washington, Idaho, and Montana; the 14th District is in Honolulu, Hawaii, and covers Hawaii, Guam, Samoa, and a large area of the Pacific Ocean; and the 17th District is in Juneau, Alaska, and covers Alaska and the Arctic Ocean.

A worker cleans oil-covered rocks with a heated water spray hose after the 1989 Exxon *Valdez* oil spill.

SEARCH AND RESCUE

Search and rescue (SAR) is one of the Coast Guard's oldest missions. Minimizing loss of life, injury, and property damage by rendering aid to persons in distress has always been a Coast Guard priority.

To meet this responsibility, the Coast Guard maintains SAR facilities on the East, West, and Gulf coasts; in Alaska, Hawaii, Guam, and Puerto Rico; and on the Great Lakes and inland U.S. waterways. The Coast Guard conducts, on average, six search-and-rescue missions a day, involving any combination of boats, cutters, and helicopters.

MEDEVACS

Medical evacuations (medevacs) are part of the Coast Guard's daily routine. On January 18, 2002, the Coast Guard evacuated fisherman Edward Williams from a crab boat in the Bering Sea. At about 9:30 P.M., Williams was working on the deck of the *Lady Kiska* when he was struck in the chest by a 700-pound (318-kg) crab pot. *Lady Kiska* radioed the Coast Guard station at Kodiak, requesting assistance. The station's duty-flight surgeon talked to the captain to determine the extent of Williams' injuries and then

Left: Attached to a winch, a Coast Guard frogman helps a stranded fisherman to the safety of a Coast Guard HH65A helicopter off the coast of Massachusetts, September 1999.

IF YOU SEE A FLARE...

To improve the Coast Guard's ability to locate a mariner in distress, a technique known as the "Fist Method" has been developed. This helps to determine accurately the position of the flare in relation to yourself.

The Fist Method

To estimate the distance of a flare from your position, the Coast Guard needs to determine the height of the flare above the horizon. To do this, hold your arm straight out in front of you, and make a closed fist. Hold the bottom of your fist on the horizon with the thumb side pointing up. Picture in your mind the flare that you saw, then compare the height of the flare at its peak to your fist. Was it a half-fist? A whole fist? Two fists?

By using this method, the Coast Guard can estimate how far away the flare is from you. The Coast Guard will ask you several more questions to narrow down the position of the flare:

What color was the flare?

How many flares did you see?

How long between the flares?

What type of flare was it? Meteor/star? Parachute? Handheld?

Where did the flare appear to come from? A boat? A plane?

What is your position?

What is the weather?

Can you assist?

What is your name?

IF YOU SHOOT A FLARE...

Flares are required equipment on boats because they could save your life. Never hesitate to shoot a flare if you are in distress or in need of assistance.

You must be aware, however, that firing a flare will bring a response from anyone who sees it. A boater will often come to assist when a flare is fired. Other boaters may also have seen the flare and called the Coast Guard.

For this reason, it is important that you let the Coast Guard know by VHF radio or phone that you have fired a flare. You must contact the Coast Guard even if you are no longer in danger or if you fired the flare accidentally. The Coast Guard can then call off any rescue forces that may be out looking for you, keeping them available to assist mariners in actual distress.

A survivor in a raft holds a lit flare. Handheld flares are useful in alerting nearby rescuers, but an airborne flare can be seen for several miles and is a more effective distress signal.

recommended that he be medevaced to the hospital in Anchorage. A Coast Guard Jayhawk helicopter was dispatched from Saint Paul at 10:47 P.M. and arrived on the scene at 11:10 P.M. The injured Williams was hoisted up and flown to Saint Paul, where he arrived in a stable condition at 11:15 P.M. A waiting ambulance took him to a clinic to await civilian air-ambulance transportation to Anchorage.

ADRIFT ON THE HIGH SEAS

In October 2001, the Coast Guard and Navy combined to locate two men and a dog drifting helplessly off Molokai. Ian Buscher, Tom Zelko, and Lucky, a black Labrador, started out on a brief 50-mile (81-km) round trip that turned into a four-day ordeal. They left Kailua, on Oahu, on October 1, bound for Molokai in a 15-foot (4.5-m) outboard skiff. They took five tubes of sunscreen and a cooler full of snacks and drinks, but no radio or compass and no safety equipment, apart from lifejackets. If they had been equipped with an emergency position-indicating beacon, a VHF-FM radio, or even flares, they could have been rescued within hours.

The crew reached the coast of Molokai, where Buscher called his wife on his cell phone to say that they had arrived and would be back by 11:30 A.M. Shortly after, an engine warning sounded. Thinking they might be low on oil, the men switched off the engine. Then, leaving the boat drifting, they went for a swim. Before long, they had drifted out of sight of land. With no compass, they were lost. Buscher and Zelko guessed that they had drifted south, but they had actually drifted northwest. They zigzagged

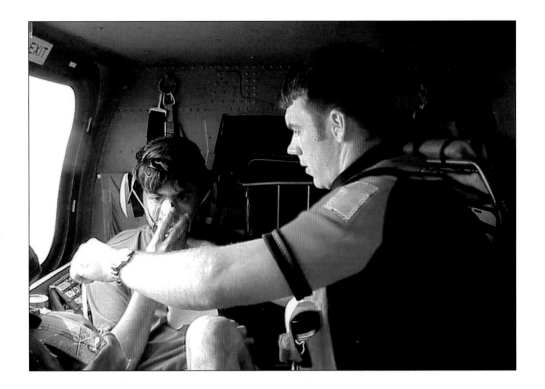

A helicopter crew from Air Station Atlantic City medevacs a man suffering from chest pains off the tanker Santa Spirit, anchored 23 miles (37 km) off Cape May. The helicopter flew through a rainstorm with only two miles (about 3 km) visibility to reach him.

north and south while creeping westward, searching vainly for land.

When the men were down to their last inch of gas, they shut down the engine and Buscher tried to call his wife, Tracy. She could hear nothing but static, making out just one word—"gas." She called the Coast Guard.

A Coast Guard helicopter was dispatched and searched the area until nightfall. With any kind of lighting—even flashlights—a boat will usually be spotted, but with no lighting, a boat is almost impossible to see in the dark, even with night-vision goggles. The men prepared for a night lost at sea.

"It was actually pretty comfortable, but a little tight and very cold,"said Zelko. "The dog was unbelievably great to have; it kept us warm." The next day, as the men made fishing lines, reflectors, and a makeshift sail, two Coast Guard HH-65 helicopters, two C-130 aircraft, a Civil Air Patrol rescue plane, and a Navy P-3 aircraft searched an area of 20,711 square miles (53,655 sq km).

As the search extended into a third and then a fourth day, Buscher

A radio direction finder aboard the Coast Guard cutter *James Rankin*. The finder uses radio frequencies to locate the position of a cutter or ship on a navigation chart.

Canadian firefighters walk away from a Canadian Coast Guard rescue helicopter at Peggy's Cove, Nova Scotia. Canadian rescue services spent many days searching the Atlantic for survivors from the crashed Swiss Air flight 111 in September 1998.

HOW TO REPORT A SEARCH-AND-RESCUE EMERGENCY

By Telephone

Look in the front of your telephone directory for an emergency number listing for the U.S. Coast Guard

or

Dial 911

or

Call your nearest U.S. Coast Guard Rescue Coordination Center. To find out your nearest center, see the Program Points of Contact page on the U.S. Coast Guard Web site (www.uscg.mil).

By VHF-FM Radio

Call for U.S. Coast Guard on Channel 16 VHF-FM (156.8 MHz)

Emergency Radio Call Procedures:

1. Make sure radio is on.

2. Select channel 16.

3. Press/hold the Transmit button.

4. Clearly say: "MAYDAY, MAYDAY, MAYDAY."

5. Also give:

    Vessel name or description

    Position or location

    Nature of emergency

    Number of people on board

6. Release Transmit button.

7. Wait 10 seconds—if there is no response, repeat "MAYDAY" call.

By Cellular Phone

VHF-FM radios are the preferred method for reporting emergencies from vessels on the water. Cellular phones are an acceptable secondary means of calling the Coast Guard.

Look in the front of your telephone directory for an emergency number listing for the U.S. Coast Guard

or

Dial *CG (only some areas and cellular providers; check to see if this service is provided in your area or with your provider)

or

Dial 911

or

Call the nearest U.S. Coast Guard Rescue Coordination Center listed on the Program Points of Contact page on the Coast Guard Web site.

By Other Methods

The Global Maritime Distress and Safety System (GMDSS) provides a number of additional means for contacting or alerting SAR authorities. These include INMARSAT, SARSAT (EPIRBs), MF-DSC, HF-DSC, and others.

In addition, vessels or persons in distress may use nationally and internationally accepted and prescribed visual and sound distress signals: flares, horns, mirrors, flashing lights, and flags.

On October 4, 2001, Ian Buscher, Tom Zelko, and Lucky the dog were finally spotted after four days adrift in the Pacific Ocean. Navy rescue swimmer Chris Haddy boarded their 15-foot (4.5-m) boat to airlift them to safety.

and Zelko were in no immediate danger. "It was beautiful, and the conditions were perfect. We were blessed, we were healthy, and we were only thinking positive things," said Buscher. The men rationed out their food, calculating on having enough for 10 days. They gave Lucky cheese crackers and water from the ice in the cooler.

At about 3:00 P.M. on October 4, the Navy P-3 suddenly spotted a blip on its radar. What had saved the men was that they had levered a piece of metal out of the boat's **knee board** and then fastened it to the top of the mast, making them detectable by radar.

As the P-3 approached the boat, Buscher and Zelko lit a makeshift smoke signal by burning a gasoline-soaked rubber boot on the end of a plank. After a search of approximately 51,000 square

A Coast Guard cutter transports floating buoys used for tracking a ship's position. In an emergency, an **EPIRBS** beacon on board a ship sends a signal via satellite giving the ship's location.

A Coast Guard Grumman Commandant seaplane. The Coast Guard first used fixed-wing support aircraft as early as 1915.

miles (132,124 sq km)—roughly the size of Louisiana—the search was over. Buscher, Zelko, and Lucky were airlifted by a Navy H-60 helicopter and taken to Marine Corps Base Hawaii in Kaneohe, where all were declared fit and healthy.

AMVER

AMVER, sponsored by the U.S. Coast Guard, is a computer-based, voluntary, ship-reporting system. It is used worldwide by search-and-rescue authorities to locate the nearest vessels to a ship in distress and divert the ships best suited to offer assistance.

Originally known as the Atlantic Vessel Emergency Reporting System, AMVER was initiated on July 18, 1958. It was confined to the north Atlantic, notorious for its icebergs, fogs, and winter storms. The Coast Guard Commandant, Vice Admiral Alfred C. Richmond, invited all U.S.- and foreign-commercial vessels of over 1,000 tons and making a voyage of over 24 hours to participate.

The system used an early computer, the IBM RAMAC (Random Access Method Accounting Control) to produce a Surface Picture (or "SURPIC") of an area of the ocean showing the location of participating ships. Within two years, AMVER's database had grown to 5,000 vessels, with an average of 770 ships "on plot" in a 24-hour period.

AMVER soon began to receive **sail plans** and position, diversion, and arrival reports from ships worldwide. Rescue centers in Britain began using search-and-rescue information from AMVER in 1962. By 1963, AMVER was plotting voyages worldwide.

In its second decade, AMVER's effectiveness was greatly helped by rapid technological progress and increasing numbers of participants. In 1967, three maritime radio stations in Spain joined the network, and by 1968, an additional 28 stations in the Atlantic and 37 in the Pacific had joined. In the 1960s and 1970s, AMVER was used to plan the emergency procedures for the *Mercury, Gemini,* and *Apollo* space missions. In 1971, AMVER's name was changed to reflect its coverage well beyond the Atlantic. As the AMVER acronym was already well-known, the decision was made to change the name to Automated, Mutual-Assistance VEssel Rescue, thus keeping the same initials.

On October 4, 1980, AMVER hit the news when it coordinated the response to an engine-room fire and flooding aboard the Dutch

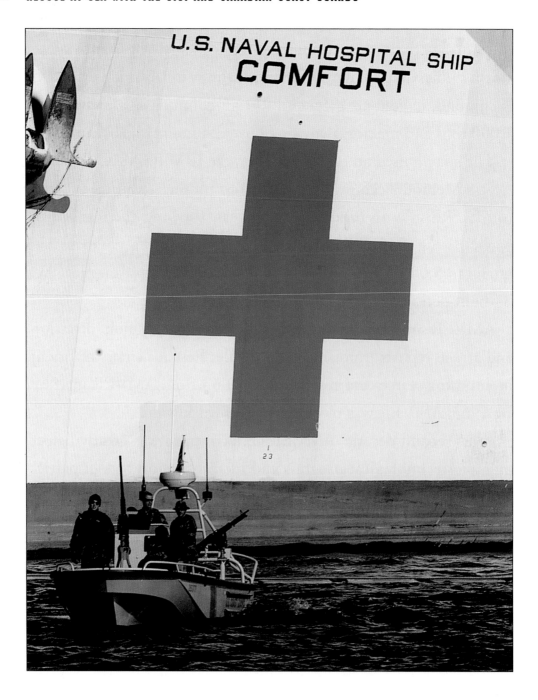

A Coast Guard gunboat stands guard over the U.S. Navy hospital ship, *Comfort*, in New York Harbor. The *U.S.S. Comfort* treated many injured people following the terrorist attack on September 11, 2001.

liner *Prinsendam*, carrying 519 passengers and crew. The tanker *Williamsburg*, the MV *Greatland*, the SS *Sohio Intrepid*, and the SS *Portland* all diverted to offer assistance. *Williamsburg* arrived in less than seven hours and took 175 survivors aboard from lifeboats, motor launches, and life rafts. One of the most important recent innovations has been the emergence of automatic distress-signaling and positioning devices. Electronic Position Indicating Radio Beacons (EPIRBS), Inmarsat-C, and Digital Select Calling auto-alarms have helped "take the search out of search and rescue." AMVER can now turn its full attention to coordinating rescues.

In 1994, six AMVER-participating ships converged on the burning Italian cruise ship *Achille Lauro* to recover the survivors. In the same year, in the largest AMVER rescue to date, 41 ships from 18 nations searched for six days to recover the only two survivors of the Ukrainian freighter *Salvador Allende*, which sank 750 miles (1,208 km) off the coast of Nova Scotia.

AMVER has continued to grow. In 1996, China joined, and a few months later, the Chinese container ship *Gao He* rescued a retired U.S. Navy captain from his stricken sailing vessel in the Pacific Ocean. Today, 12,000 ships from over 140 nations partici-pate in AMVER. An average of 2,800 ships are "on plot" each day, and AMVER tracks over 100,000 voyages annually. More than 2,000 lives have been saved by AMVER-participating ships in the last 10 years.

AMVER is a illustration of international humanitarian coopera-tion, mariner helping mariner, by assisting any vessel in distress, regardless of nationality. Participation is voluntary and free.

DRUGS AND IMMIGRATION

The Coast Guard is the leading federal agency for maritime drug interdiction and shares responsibility for air interdiction with the U.S. Customs Service. As the primary maritime law-enforcement agency, the Coast Guard is also responsible for enforcing immigration law at sea.

DRUG INTERDICTIONS

The Coast Guard's mission is to reduce the supply of drugs from their source by denying them access to the Transit Zone, an area covering 6 million square miles (15,544,041 sq km) and including the Caribbean, Gulf of Mexico, and eastern Pacific. Over this vast area, the Coast Guard frequently cooperates with other federal agencies as well as other countries in the region to disrupt the flow of illegal drugs.

The Revenue Cutter Service was first employed in preventing drug smuggling in 1870, when Chinese sailors smuggled opium into the United States in merchant ship cargoes and baggage. Although there was some smuggling of cocaine and marijuana in the early 20th century, the modern phase of intensive drug smuggling began in the

Left: The Coast Guard rescuing passengers from a stricken Haitian immigrant boat. Immigrant interdictions can often turn into rescue operations in the dangerous waters of the Caribbean.

early 1970s. The Coast Guard conducted its first drug seizure on March 8, 1973, when the Coast Guard cutter *Dauntless* boarded a 38-foot (12-m) sports fisherman boat, *Big L*, and arrested its crew in possession of almost a ton of marijuana. Since then, the Coast Guard has made countless drug seizures. In the year 2000, the Coast Guard seized over 100,000 tons of cocaine and 50,000 tons of marijuana, with a street value of over $4 billion. The Coast Guard is at the forefront of the fight against drug smuggling and cooperates extensively with agencies such as the Drug Enforcement Agency.

Crew of the CGC *Tampa* with some of the drugs haul seized on January 10, 2001, in the Bahamas. *Tampa* and three other cutters intercepted a go-fast loaded with 5,000 lbs (2,270 kg) of marijuana.

On May 14, 2001, Coast Guard officers stand guard over 13 tons of cocaine found aboard the Belize-registered fishing boat *Svesda Maru* off San Diego in the largest maritime cocaine bust in U.S. history.

DRUG SEIZURE STATISTICS

Year	1994	1995	1996	1997	1998	1999	2000
Cocaine	47,333	33,629	28,585	103,617	82,623	111,689	132,920
Marijuana	33,895	40,164	31,000	102,538	31,390	61,506	50,463
Cases	67	44	36	122	129	118	92
Vessels seized	28	34	41	64	75	74	56
Arrests	73	56	23	233	297	302	201
Value seized	$1.8 bn	$1.3 bn	$1.1 bn	$4.0 bn	$3.0 bn	$3.7 bn	$4.4 bn

IMMIGRANT INTERDICTIONS

The Coast Guard intercepts illegal immigrants at sea before they can reach the United States, making it easier and less expensive to return them to their countries of origin. Illegal immigrants from all over the world attempt to enter the country by sea, the majority coming from Haiti, Cuba, the Dominican Republic, and China.

In immigrant interdictions, the Coast Guard's first concern is preventing loss of life at sea. Many immigrant boats are unseaworthy or dangerously overloaded. According to Border Patrol

On July 4, 1994, Coast Guard personnel from the CGC *Hamilton* recover their rescue swimmer and several Haitian migrants from the water after their 40-foot (12-m) boat capsized in the Windward Passage off the coast of Haiti.

Haitian migrants who have been interdicted at sea are loaded onto a Coast Guard boat near Haiti on November 15, 1991. The boats used by immigrants are often dangerous and without the intervention of the Coast Guard, many lives might be lost.

figures, over 150 Cubans and Haitians have drowned trying to reach the United States since 1993.

An immigrant interdiction can often turn into a rescue operation, as happened in the "Mariel Boatlift" of 1980. In that year, Cuban president Fidel Castro allowed anyone who wanted to do so to leave Cuba. They left from Mariel Harbor, and over 100,000 migrants left between April and September. The Coast Guard conducted numerous search-and-rescue operations in U.S. and international waters. It was also occupied in preventing boats from traveling to Cuba to pick up immigrants, in violation of U.S. law.

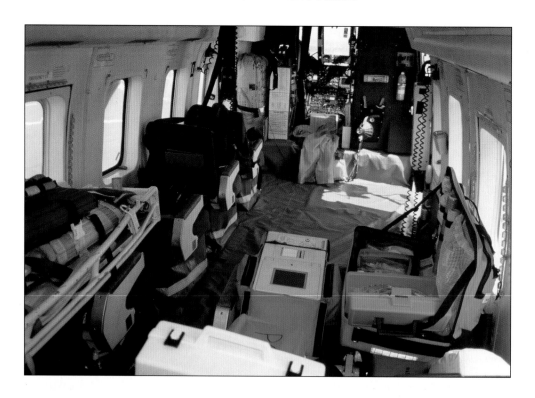

The Sikorsky S61-N helicopter is used by the Canadian Coast Guard in search-and-rescue operations. It is equipped with a first aid kit, life rafts, inflatable life vests, weather radar, and a crash-activated emergency locator transmitter.

Waves of seaborne immigration often follow political unrest in a neighboring country. In these cases, many immigrants try to reach the United States illegally, fleeing from political persecution and torture in their own countries to seek protection.

Following the 1990 **coup** in Haiti, hundreds of illegal immigrants attempted to enter the United States. There were so many applications for **asylum** that immigrants were first interviewed on Coast Guard and Navy ships, and then at the U.S. military base at Guantanamo Bay, Cuba. At one point, the base contained over

12,000 immigrants for processing.

Immigrants seeking political asylum are transferred by the Coast Guard to the Immigration and Naturalization Service (INS) for assessment. **Economic migrants** are sent home, while the others remain until their cases are investigated. Successful applicants may eventually be allowed to reside in the United States.

THE ELÍAN GONZALEZ STORY

On Thanksgiving Day (November 25), 1999, five-year-old Elían Gonzalez was found floating on an inner tube off the Florida coast after the boat taking him from Cuba sank, killing his mother and 10 other people.

Earlier that day, the only other survivors, a

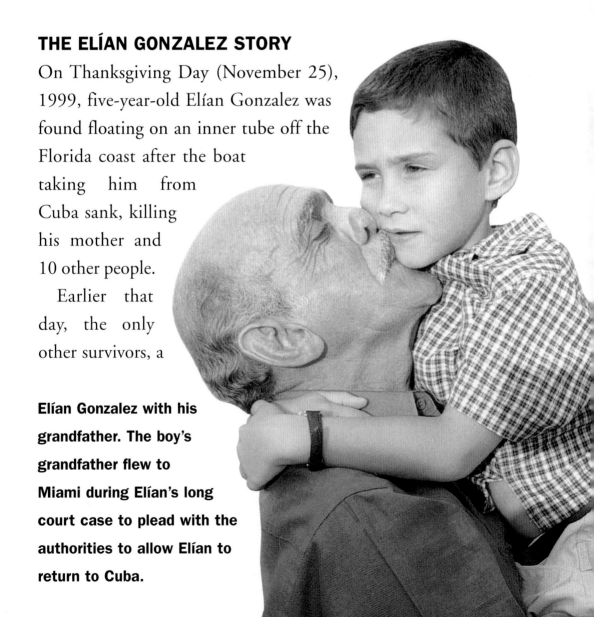

Elían Gonzalez with his grandfather. The boy's grandfather flew to Miami during Elían's long court case to plead with the authorities to allow Elían to return to Cuba.

DRUGS SEIZED IN HIGH-SPEED CHASE NEAR CUBA

On June 16, 2001, Coast Guard cutter *Monhegan* seized 3,000 lb (1,360 kg) of marijuana, a "**go-fast**" vessel, and its five-member crew after a high-speed chase and gunfire battle at sea.

A helicopter from Coast Guard Air Station Clearwater spotted the go-fast near Cuba and reported its position to the *Monhegan*, which was near the Windward Passage on the eastern end of Cuba.

An Air Station Clearwater C-130 airplane diverted to the scene to assist in tracking the go-fast. The C-130 spotted the go-fast rounding the eastern tip of Cuba and tracked it covertly from international airspace as it followed the coast of Cuba at high speed.

When the go-fast altered course toward the Bahamas, the C-130 radioed the *Monhegan*, which intercepted it 22 miles (35 km) north of Los Angeles, Cuba. The crew refused to stop, and the *Monhegan* fired numerous shots across the go-fast's bow. The men eventually gave themselves up and the *Monhegan's* crew boarded the go-fast. The master of the vessel claimed Bahamian registry, but the Coast Guard contacted the Bahamian authorities and found this was not so. In fact, the boat was unregistered—in other words, it was a boat without a nation.

A search of the vessel revealed approximately 3,000 lb (1,360 kg) of marijuana bales. The crew were detained, and the boat and its contents impounded. Three days later, the *Monhegan* delivered boat, its contents, and crew to U.S. Customs officials at its home port of Key West, Florida.

In 1999, the U.S. Coast Guard unveiled its latest helicopter, the MH90 Enforcer. The helicopter carries an inflatable boat which is designed to pursue fast drug smuggling boats.

33-year-old man and a 22-year-old woman, had been found clinging to an inner tube off the coast of Key Biscayne, Florida. The sunburned and dehydrated pair told how they were among 14 people who had left the Cuban port of Cardenas in a 16-foot (5-m) boat. On the morning of November 23, the boat sank. Seven passengers, including Elían's mother, drowned, and the survivors clung to a pair of inner tubes.

The Coast Guard, Marine Patrol units, and police officers spent the rest of Thanksgiving Day searching the area off Key Biscayne for more survivors. Two fishermen spotted Elían off the coast of Fort

Lauderdale—about 40 miles (64 km) from where the other two survivors were found. They saw what they thought was a dummy strapped to an inner tube. "We thought it was a joke," one of the fishermen said. "We said, 'Let's go by again,' and as we went by the second time…it looked like something moved."

Elían was taken to Joe DiMaggio Children's Hospital in Fort Lauderdale, suffering from dehydration. Elían made a full recovery and was allowed to stay with his great-uncle in Little Havana, Miami, while his case was considered.

However, Elían's story had barely begun. Elían's American relatives claimed he was better off with them and applied for custody of him. Elían's Cuban relatives disagreed, and flew to the United States to plead with the authorities to return Elían to his father back home.

The dispute sparked mass demonstrations in Florida and Cuba, with each side accusing the other of using Elían as a political tool. Eventually, after a long court case, it was decided that the best option for Elían was to be with his father in Cuba. Elían's father, Juan Miguel Gonzalez, flew to the United States on April 6, 2000 to take him home. Anti-Castro supporters attempted to stop Elían from being taken away, and some ugly scenes ensued. However, in the early hours of April 22, federal agents stormed the house and took Elían to his father to begin his journey back to his home country.

Left: Elían Gonzalez, the little Cuban boy rescued off the coast of Florida. He spent six months with relatives in Miami before the courts decided it was best for him to be returned home to his father.

PROTECTING NATURAL RESOURCES

The U.S. marine environment is a valuable natural resource that contributes food for millions and income running into billions of dollars, as well as pleasure and recreation for all.

The **biomass** of the U.S. Exclusive Economic Zone (EEZ) is a renewable resource, but it is not infinite and it is under threat. Over-fishing and poaching are the main culprits. A recent United Nations Food and Agriculture Organization report estimated that there is a **sustainable** 88-million-ton (80-million-metric-ton) catch available worldwide, yet in 1997, over 90 million tons (81.6 metric tons) were harvested. The Coast Guard's fisheries law-enforcement mission is vital in protecting this sensitive marine environment. The Coast Guard pursues a three-pronged approach: prevention, enforcement, and response.

Coast Guard cutters patrol closed fishing grounds off New England to let depleted species return to harvestable levels. In the Bering Sea, cutters prevent foreign vessels from poaching in fish-rich

Left: The Polar-class icebreaker *Polar Star* cuts through sea ice in the Antarctic Ocean, breaking a channel to resupply the scientific base in the Ross Sea. *Polar Star* is also a scientific research platform, with five laboratories and room for 20 scientists.

In September 2000, officers from Grand Isle Coast Guard Station, Louisiana, release a Hawksbill turtle back into the sea. The turtle, named "Very Lucky," had been found in a cargo net off Galveston, Texas, in October 1999.

Alaskan waters, and in the Pacific Ocean, Coast Guard vessels stop the illegal use of high-seas drift nets.

ENDANGERED SPECIES

The Coast Guard enforces a wide variety of fishery regulations designed to reduce the bycatch of threatened and endangered species. In the Gulf of Mexico, the Coast Guard protects endangered sea turtles from being caught in indiscriminate fishing nets. It also operates missions to protect the Hawaiian monk seal, stellar sea lion, Kemp's Ridley sea turtle, and harbor porpoise. Coast Guard vessels and aircraft patrol national marine sanctuaries and other protected areas, and enforce mandatory speed-zone regulations.

Working closely with federal, state, and nongovernmental and foreign agencies, the Coast Guard is an active steward of the world's oceans. The Coast Guard's role goes far beyond enforcement of fisheries regulations. One of many examples is the Coast Guard's role in the preservation of the northern right whale. Along the Atlantic coast, Coast Guard units free endangered whales that have become entangled in fishing gear. The Coast Guard also operates a ship-

Scientists from the CGC *Polar Star* deploying research equipment in the Antarctic. *Polar Star* scientists carry out scientific experiments in geology, vulcanology, oceanography, and sea-ice physics.

reporting system to track the whales. This ship-reporting system has the distinction of being the only one in the world dedicated to a single species.

CATCHING AN ILLEGAL DRIFT-NET BOAT

On May 16, 2001, the Coast Guard, Russian Northeast Regional Directorate, and Federal Border Service teamed up to seize an illegal drift-net vessel.

A Coast Guard C-130 aircraft from Air Station Kodiak, Alaska, spotted the Russian vessel *Sakhfrakt 3* fishing 15 miles (24 km) inside the Russian Exclusive Economic Zone and led the vessel's interception. The boat was equipped with five illegal drift nets, totaling about 17 miles (27 km) in length.

After the seizure of the boat, Coast Guard 17th District Commander Rear Admiral Tom Barrett and his Russian counter-part, Lieutenant General Nikolai Lisinsky, praised the way their two countries had worked together. Commander Barrett said that the discovery and interception of the illegal vessel was outstanding proof of the importance of cooperation in protecting valuable living marine resources.

WATER POLLUTION

The Coast Guard is a pioneer in the fight against water pollution. The Coast Guard's Research and Development Center recently perfected a technique to "fingerprint" oil to identify the source of a spill. This is essential when pollution comes from an unknown source or when polluters flee the scene of a spill.

In the Gulf of Maine, in August 1999, the Coast Guard assist in freeing an entangled humpback whale. The humpback whale is an endangered species with an estimated population of only 10,000 to 15,000 still remaining.

The Coast Guard also maintains three National Strike Teams, on call 24 hours a day, to respond to accidents and spills in the marine environment. The service also enforces federal regulations against the dumping of refuse and sewage at sea.

The Coast Guard works with foreign governments and international agencies to reduce the number of marine accidents and, therefore, the number of spills. The Coast Guard also works with the maritime industry to develop new safety standards, and conducts detailed investigations into marine accidents and spills.

AQUATIC NUISANCE SPECIES

Aquatic nuisance species (ANS) are non-native species that threaten the survival of native marine environments. They can damage marine environments, affect water and food supplies, and adversely affect human health. Unlike other forms of pollution, a nonindigenous species, once established, is here to stay.

Most nonindigenous aquatic species enter the United States in a ship's ballast water. To comply with the National Invasive Species Act of 1996, the Coast Guard enforces regulations prohibiting ships from venting their **ballast** in U.S. waters.

Nonindigenous aquatic nuisance plants, such as purple loosestrife, Eurasian watermilfoil, and hydrilla, quickly establish themselves and replace native plants. Dense growths of these weeds lead to degradation of water quality, accelerated filling of lakes and reservoirs, impairment of navigation, and destruction of recreation areas. ANS invasions can also pose serious health risks. In 1991, a South American strain of the human cholera bacteria was found in the ballast tanks of ships in the port of Mobile, Alabama. Cholera strains were also found in oyster and finfish samples in Mobile Bay.

The ANS with the biggest impact on U.S. waters is probably the zebra mussel, found in the Great Lakes. Zebra mussels consume large quantities of microscopic plants and animals, depleting the food sources of native species and disturbing the whole aquatic food chain. They reproduce quickly and cause profound ecological changes in the Great Lakes and rivers of central North America.

In Honolulu, Hawaii, in November 1999, a crew member aboard the CGC *Walnut* offloads some of the 57,000 lbs (26,000 kg) of debris cleared off coral reefs used by the Hawaiian monk seal in the northwest Hawaiian Islands.

These efforts have been successful. Oil spills have decreased by 75 percent since 1993—from 6.7 gallons (24 liters) spilled per million gallons shipped in 1996 to only 1.2 gallons (4.4 million liters) spilled in 2000.

OIL SPILLS

Until passage of the Federal Water Pollution Control Act (FWPCA) in 1972, federal enforcement of water pollution regulations was based upon requirements of the Refuse Act of 1899 and the Oil Pollution Act of 1924.

Neither of these required extensive reporting or record-keeping. Many spills went unreported, and it was hard to take preventive steps without accurate information on the size, type, and causes of the spills.

In March 1967, the tanker *Torrey Canyon* wrecked on the south coast of England, discharging her entire cargo of crude oil into the English Channel. This incident focused international attention on the problem of massive oil pollution from tanker incidents. Then, in 1968, there was a huge oil-well blowout in the Santa Barbara Channel off the coast of California.

These two incidents eventually led to the passage of the Federal Water Pollution Control Act (FWPCA) in 1972 and to international adoption of the International Convention for the Prevention

Right: In Indian Creek, Maryland, response crewmen offload a soiled boom as part of the cleanup efforts after a faulty pipeline leaked 111,000 gallons (505,000 liters) of oil into Swanson Creek.

of Pollution from Ships (MARPOL) in 1973. The FWPCA, also known as the Clean Water Act, gave the Coast Guard authority to regulate oil pollution prevention and response in U.S. waterways. The Act requires any discharge of oil or hazardous substance in a harmful quantity to be reported to the "appropriate agency of the United States." The Coast Guard was designated the "appropriate agency" on August 3, 1973.

As it was now compulsory to report spills, the number of spills

A Coast Guard HC-130 Hercules prepares for takeoff. The Hercules is a long-range surveillance and transport, fixed-wing aircraft that is used to perform a wide variety of missions, including transporting supplies and equipment.

The Canadian Coast Guard icebreaker *Louis S. St-Laurent* cuts through the winter ice in the Gulf of St. Lawrence. This ship is capable of extended operations in the most extreme conditions.

reported increased dramatically, and the Coast Guard was able to get a full picture of the problem of oil pollution for the first time. They began building a spills database, now known as the Marine Safety Management System (MSMS), at Coast Guard Headquarters in Washington, D.C. This information helps them discover the causes of spills, identify the polluters, and take steps to prevent future spills.

Spill reports, as required by the FWPCA, are usually made by the private parties or government agencies involved in the incident. In a few cases, polluters flee the scene and reports have to be made by Coast Guard officers who discover the spill.

THE U.S. COAST GUARD AT WAR

The Coast Guard, and its predecessor, the Revenue Cutter Service, has served in every major war fought by the United States. At the time of the founding of the United States, there was no Navy and the revenue cutters were the only maritime force.

Cutters were soon involved in military affairs. In 1794, the cutter *Virginia* arrested the crew of *Unicorn*, which was being outfitted as a privateer in support of the French republic. Cutters also intervened to impose U.S. neutrality during the Napoleonic Wars.

After the formation of the U.S. Navy, laws were passed making the Coast Guard part of the Navy in time of war or whenever the president directs. The Act of March 2, 1799, stated that the cutters "shall, whenever the President of the United States shall so direct, cooperate with the Navy of the United States, during which time they shall be under the direction of the Secretary of the Navy."

THE QUASI-WAR WITH FRANCE (1797–1801)

In the Quasi-War with France, eight cutters operated along the southern coast and in the Caribbean. Eighteen of the 22

Left: A Coast Guard officer guarding a naval compound in Saudi Arabia during Operation Desert Storm. Coast Guard units were deployed to the Gulf to carry out coastal patrol, antiterrorism, and port security operations.

ships captured by the U.S. between 1798 and 1799 were taken by unaided cutters, and two by cutters assisting the Navy. The cutter *Pickering* captured 10 ships, one of which carried 44 guns and was manned by some 200 sailors, more than three times the strength of the Pickering.

THE WAR OF 1812

At the start of the War of 1812, Treasury Secretary Albert Gallatin requested from Congress "small, fast sailing vessels," because there were "but six vessels belonging to the Navy under the size of frigates." Shallow-draft cutters supplemented the Navy and fought extensively in U.S. coastal waters.

The defense of the cutter *Eagle* against the attack of the British **brig** *Dispatch* and another ship is one of the most dramatic incidents of the war. *Eagle* ran ashore on Long Island, and its crew dragged their guns onto a hill to defend the position. The crew fought the British all day. When they ran out of shot for their guns, they prized out the enemy's shot that was lodged in the hill and fired it back. During the battle, *Eagle's* flag was shot away three times, and each time, a volunteer replaced it.

THE WAR WITH MEXICO (1846–1848)

The two principal naval operations carried out in the War with Mexico were blockading Mexican coasts and making amphibious landings. The Navy needed shallow-draft vessels for these landings and made use of five cutters. Cutters were vital in a number of landings, particularly those at Alvarado and Tabasco.

The cutter *Eagle*, which ran aground on Long Island in the War of 1812. *Eagle*'s crew bravely defended their position against the British in a day-long battle.

THE AMERICAN CIVIL WAR (1861–1865)

The sympathies of the cutter forces were divided during the Civil War, with some of them joining the Confederacy. Members of the cutter *Robert McLelland* defected to the Confederacy while the ship was at New Orleans Harbor, prompting the Treasury Secretary to send a famous dispatch to General John A. Dix, declaring:

Admiral W.F. Sampson's fleet of cutters after their victory at the Battle of Santiago in the Spanish-American War of 1898.

"If anyone attempts to haul down the American flag, shoot him on sight." In the Civil War, the main duties of Union cutters were patrolling for commerce raiders and providing fire support for troops on shore. Confederate cutters were mainly used as commerce raiders. Cutters were involved in some notable individual actions. The first naval shot fired in the Civil War was by the cutter *Harriet Lane* when it challenged the steamer *Nashville,* attempting to enter Charleston Harbor without flying a U.S. flag. *Harriet Lane* also took part in the capture of Hatteras Inlet, and after that was transferred to the Navy.

The cutter *Miami* carried President Abraham Lincoln to Fort Monroe at the start of the Peninsular Campaign. In December 1862, the cutter *Hercules* battled Confederate forces on the Rappahannock River. On April 21, 1865, cutters were ordered to search all outbound ships for the assassins of President Lincoln.

THE SPANISH–AMERICAN WAR (1898)

Eight cutters were in Admiral Sampson's fleet and on the Havana blockade. In the naval action off Cardenas on May 11, 1898, the cutter *Hudson* fought side-by-side with the Navy torpedo boat USS *Winslow*. When half of *Winslow's* crew was killed in the battle, *Hudson* came to *Winslow's* aid and rescued the remaining crew. In recognition of this act of heroism, Congress awarded a gold medal to *Hudson's* commander, Lieutenant Frank H. Newcomb, a silver medal to each of the officers, and a bronze medal to each of the enlisted men.

WORLD WAR I (1914–1918)

Cutters enforced U.S. neutrality at the beginning of World War I. In 1915, the service joined with the Life-Saving Service to form the Coast Guard. After the United States declared war on Germany on April 6, 1917, the Coast Guard's 47 vessels were transferred to the Navy for active service.

In August and September 1917, six cutters—*Ossipee, Seneca, Yamacraw, Algonquin, Manning,* and *Tampa*—joined the U.S. Atlantic Fleet, based in Gibraltar. Throughout the rest of the war, they escorted hundreds of vessels between Gibraltar and the British

Isles. Other cutters performed escort duties off Bermuda, in the Azores, in the Caribbean, and off the coast of Nova Scotia.

Tampa escorted 18 convoys between Gibraltar and the British Isles. On the evening of September 26, 1918, *Tampa* was making for the port of Milford Haven, Wales. At 8:45 P.M., the convoy heard a loud explosion. U.S. and British ships searched the area, finding nothing but some wreckage and two unidentified bodies in Navy uniforms. Although it was never fully confirmed, a German U-53 reported sinking a U.S. warship fitting *Tampa's* description that night. The entire crew of 115, of whom 111 were Coast Guard personnel, were lost.

WORLD WAR II (1939–1945)

After the United States entered World War II in 1941, Coast Guard cutters were assigned to the Navy. The Coast Guard's duties included search and rescue, port security, and operating the Greenland Patrol. Coast Guard personnel also served on Navy battleships.

One of the Coast Guard's most important duties was amphibious troop transportation. The Coast Guard was involved in every important invasion of the war: in North Africa, Italy, France, and the Pacific, and trained the other forces in the use of amphibious craft.

In U.S. waters, the Coast Guard patrolled for submarines and rescued more than 1,500 survivors of torpedo attacks. Cutters on escort duty saved 1,000 more lives, and 1,500 more were rescued during the Normandy landings. During World War II, 230,000 men and 10,000 women served in the Coast Guard, suffering 1,918 casualties.

Dropping depth charges in the Atlantic. Over 200,000 Coast Guard members served in World War II, many of them joining the crews of U.S. Navy vessels in combat.

THE KOREAN WAR (1950–1953)

In the Korean War, the Coast Guard was responsible for troop transportation, search and rescue, port security, ammunition handling, weather stations, and long-range navigation. Coast Guard bases were established across the Pacific to support UN troop transports in the Philippines, Guam, Wake, Midway, Adak, and Barbers Point in the Hawaiian Islands. About 50 Coast Guard personnel were also stationed in Korea and helped to establish the Korean Coast Guard, which has since evolved into their navy.

A COAST GUARD PHOTOGRAPHER AT D-DAY

In 1944, 25-year-old Coast Guard photographer George Durenberger was photographing cadets at the Coast Guard Academy when he was transferred to the USS *Joseph T. Dickman*, bound for Europe.

"Like a lot of other guys, I thought Coast Guard meant exactly that: guarding the coast," says Durenberger. "Nobody told you the Coast Guard would be going to Europe, Africa, or wherever." Upon arrival, Dickman's crew began D-Day training. "We would go out and practice landings for Normandy. Of course, at that time, we didn't know where we were going."

On the morning of June 6, 1944, the *Dickman* joined the historic fleet containing 1,200 fighting ships, 10,000 planes, 4,126 landing craft, 804 transport ships, and hundreds of amphibious tanks. More than 130,000 Allied troops landed on the Normandy coast.

The Germans were ready, bombarding the Allied soldiers from over 9,000 fortified positions. Sustaining heavy casualties, Allied troops eventually pushed the Germans back and took the beaches.

"The German soldiers were hidden...behind a hill," Durenberger recalls. "All you could hear was a lot of shooting. The fire was very heavy." Durenberger shot stills and film footage of the operation. That evening, disoriented by the fury of the battle, he somehow found himself on a troop ship full of wounded soldiers bound for the *Dickman*. Durenberger's pictures were published back home in the U.S., one of them appearing on the cover of *Life* magazine.

George Durenberger at home today showing off the camera he used as a 25-year-old Coast Guard photographer to capture the action of the 1944 D-Day landings in Normandy.

Coast Guard members as part of the U.S. fleet in the Persian Gulf during Operation Desert Storm in 1991. The Coast Guard was among the first U.S. forces sent to the Gulf at the beginning of the conflict.

THE VIETNAM WAR (1965–1975)

At the start of the military buildup, the Navy lacked shallow-draft craft for inshore operations. The Coast Guard sent 26 cutters to Vietnam, forming Squadron One, stationed at Danang, Cat La, and An Thai. The cutters inspected **junks** for contraband, intercepted and destroyed North Vietnamese and Viet Cong craft, and provided fire support. Later, the Coast Guard sent 30 deep-water cutters to guard the oceans.

Since most munitions entered South Vietnam by sea, the Army asked the Coast Guard to control harbor security and transportation. Coast Guard officers inspected ports for security against attack and supervised the safe storage and loading of explosives.

In 1966, the Coast Guard set up and operated a LORAN C long-range navigation system to assist warplanes in precise navigation, with stations in Thailand at Lampang, Sattahip, and Udorn; and in Vietnam at Con Son and Tan My.

Coast Guard pilots also flew combat search-and-rescue missions with the Air Force, mostly with the 37th Aerospace Rescue and Recovery Squadron at Danang.

THE GULF WAR (1990–1991)

At the beginning of the Persian Gulf crisis, Coast Guard law enforcement boarding teams, experienced in boarding drug vessels, were deployed on naval vessels to assist in enforcing UN sanctions against Iraq. After war broke out, these teams handled the first Iraqi prisoners of war.

In the first involuntary mobilization of the Coast Guard Reserve in its 50-year history, Reserve Port Security Units from Milwaukee, Buffalo, and Cleveland were sent to the Middle East to carry out coastal patrol, antiterrorism, and port security operations.

On April 20, 1991, the Coast Guard's raider boat, with a crew of six, was the first Allied vessel to enter the harbor of Kuwait City after the country's liberation. After the war, the Coast Guard led an international team to assist in the cleanup of the massive oil spill created by Iraq in the Persian Gulf.

GLOSSARY

Arms: weapons

Asylum: refuge offered to immigrants fleeing danger or persecution in their homelands

Ballast: heavy objects or substance used to improve the stability and control of a ship

Biomass: the total amount of living matter in a particular area

Bow: the front of a boat or ship; the back is known as the stern

Breeches buoy: a pair of rigid breeches attached to the underside of a life buoy; shipwreck survivors climb in and are hoisted to a ship or helicopter

Brig: short for brigantine, a two-masted square-rigged ship

Contraband: illegally gained goods

Coup: a sudden and successful act or strike

Cutter: any craft over 65 feet (20 m) in length with accommodation for a crew

Dory: a flat-bottomed boat with high, flaring sides

Driftnet: huge nets, 1–56 miles (2–90 km) in length, made of fine nylon mesh and used to fish for tuna, salmon, and squid

Economic migrant: a migrant who is not being persecuted in his home, but leaves his country simply to make more money abroad

Federalize: to bring something under the control of central government

Go-fast: a small, fast, maneuverable boat, used by drug smugglers to outrun the Coast Guard

Hove to: to turn your vessel so it is facing another vessel

Interdiction: an operation to divert or arrest lawbreakers such as drug smugglers

Junk: a low-lying Chinese vessel used for transporting goods along coastal waters

Jurisdiction: the power to exercise authority

Materiel: equipment and supplies used by an armed force

Nonindigenous: non-native

Privateer: an armed private ship that acts against the ships or commerce of an enemy; often called "pirates"

Prohibition: a period in the 1920s where alcohol was banned in the United States

Sail plan: a report of a ship's intended journey, which is lodged before sailing and lists the course, departure and arrival times, and details of the vessel, cargo, and crew

Sustainable: the sustainable catch in a marine area is the maximum amount that can be caught without the danger of depleting future stocks

Tariff: a tax paid for bringing goods into a country

UN: the United Nations; an international organization where nations can come together to discuss issues and make decisions

CHRONOLOGY

1789: The service eventually to be known as the U.S. Lighthouse Service, is established under the control of the Treasury Department (1 Stat. L. 53).

1790: Congress passes 1 Stat. L. 145, 175 creating the "system of cutters," controlled by the Treasury Department; later called the Revenue Service, and Revenue Marine, it is officially named the Revenue Cutter Service (12 Stat. L., 639) in 1863.

1848: Congress appropriates funds to pay for life-saving equipment to be used by volunteer organizations (9 Stat. L. 321, 322).

1852: Steamboat Act establishes Steamboat Inspection Service under the control of the Treasury Department (10 Stat. L., 1852).

1878: Life-Saving Service established as a separate agency under the control of the Treasury Department (20 Stat. L., 163).

1884: Bureau of Navigation established under the control of the Treasury Department (23 Stat. L., 118).

1903: Department of Commerce and Labor is created (32 Stat. L., 825), with control of the Bureau of Navigation and the Steamship Inspection Service.

1915: Life-Saving Service and Revenue Cutter Service are combined to form the Coast Guard (38 Stat. L., 800).

1917: With the declaration of war against Germany, the Coast Guard is transferred by Executive Order to the control of the Navy Department.

1919: Coast Guard reverts to Treasury Department with President Wilson's Executive Order 3160.

1932: Steamboat Inspection Service and Bureau of Navigation are combined to form the Bureau of Navigation and Steamboat Inspection (47 Stat. L., 415).

1936: Public Law 622 combines the Bureau of Navigation and Steamboat Inspection Service to form the Bureau of Marine Inspection and Navigation (49 Stat. L., 1380).

1939: Lighthouse Service becomes part of the Coast Guard (53 Stat. L., 1432).

1941: President Roosevelt's Executive Order 8929 transfers the Coast Guard to Navy Department control.

1946: In compliance with Executive Order 9666, the Coast Guard is returned to Treasury Department control; Coast Guard creates the Eastern, Western, and Pacific Area commands.

1946: The Bureau of Marine Inspection becomes part of the Coast Guard.

1967: Executive Order 167–81 transfers the Coast Guard to the newly formed Department of Transportation.

FURTHER INFORMATION

USEFUL WEB SITES

For the U.S. Coast Guard, see: www.uscg.mil;
www.uscg.mil/hq/g-cp/cb/CGMagazine.shtm;
www.cga.edu; www.cgaux.org/cgauxweb/public/pubframe.htm

For the Canadian Coast Guard, see: ccg-gcc.gc.ca

For environmental issues, see: www.earthtrust.org/dnw.html

For the Oil Spill Intelligence Report, see: http://cutter.com/osir

FURTHER READING

Canney, Donald L. *Rum War: The U.S. Coast Guard and Prohibition.* Washington: U.S. Coast Guard, 1990.

Capelotti, Pete. *Oceanography in the Coast Guard.* Washington: Coast Guard Historian's Office, 1996.

Farson, Robert H. *Twelve Men Down: Massachusetts Sea Rescues.* Yarmouth Port, Massachusetts: Cape Cod Historical Publications, 2000.

Fuss, Charles M., Jr. *Sea of Grass: The Maritime Drug War, 1970–1990.* Annapolis: Naval Institute Proceedings, 1996.

Gottschalk, Jack A., and Brian P. Flanagan. *Jolly Roger with an Uzi: The Rise and Threat of Modern Piracy.* Annapolis: NIP, 2000.

Junger, Sebastian. *The Perfect Storm: A True Story of Men against the Sea.* New York: Harper Paperbacks, 1998.

Larzelere, Alex. *The Coast Guard at War: Vietnam, 1965–1975.* Annapolis, Maryland: Naval Institute Press, 1997.

Shanks, Ralph, and Wick York. *The U.S. Life-Saving Service: Heroes, Rescues and Architecture of the Early Coast Guard.* Petaluma, California: Costano Books, 1996.

Walker, Spike. *Coming Back Alive: The Most Harrowing Search and Rescue Mission Ever Attempted on Alaska's High Seas.* New York: St. Martin's Press, 2001.

ABOUT THE AUTHOR

Lewis Lyons is a freelance author and journalist based in London, England, who has written on everything from business law to sewage. He was educated at Oxford University and the University of London and started his career working for a London community newspaper. He spent seven years in the United States, for the most part in New York City, where he headed a photo agency, edited a computer magazine, and wrote on technology, music, business, culture, and society. His recent publications include books and articles on the Internet, the soccer World Cup, and 20th-century ceremonial dress. He is currently writing on topics as diverse as travel, earth sciences, language, and music.

INDEX

References in italics refer to illustrations